HOW To MARRY A MILLIONAIRE

RACHITA KUMAR

COPYRIGHT

This Electronic book is Copyright © 2019 By Rachita Kumar. All rights are reserved. No part of this book may be reproduced, stored in a retrieval system, or transmitted by any means; electronic, mechanical, photocopying, recording, or otherwise, without written permission from the copyright holder(s).

Table of Contents

Introduction 1

Understanding The Principles 4

  1. You don't have to make millions to be able to attract a millionaire. 4

  2. It is true, that men fall in love with their eyes first. 5

  3. Unfortunately you have a short age window to marry a millionaire. 5

  4. Wealthy men love beautiful women. 6

  5. Your beauty will help to attract a millionaire, but your brain will help you to keep him. 6

  6. Make sure that you know etiquette and use it in your daily life at all times. 7

  7. You have to learn all about dress codes and a proper makeup. 7

  8. When you feel confident and ready to meet your destiny, don't leave it up to fate. 8

  9. And the last, but most important fact about marrying a millionaire: 8

THE PLAN 10

  Use Your Brains 12

  Use Your Body 14

Work on Your Social Skills and Personality. 15

Sex – How to Use It? 16

Location, Location, Location (maters) 16

Know What You Are Looking At 19

Beware of Your Competition 20

Do NOT Be Yourself 20

Speak the Language of the Rich 21

Physically Prepare Yourself 22

Get in Early 22

Observe the Rich 23

How To Choose The Datting Site That Meets Your Expectations 26

How to choose the best dating site 27

27 YEARS INFLUENCIER WHO MARRIED A 57 YEARS MILLIONAIRE 31

Where to find the Rich? 35

Millionaire Match Making Websites 37

Getting to Know Each Other 39

Habits and Traits and Millionaires 40

KIM REINVENTED HERSELF WITH THE SOLE AIM OF LANDING A RICH HUSBAND - AND GOT ONE 48

What Are the Goal Setting to Marry a Millionaire 57

Definition of a Goal 58

WOMAN MARRIES ONLINE BOYFRIEND WITHIN
10MONTHS AND FINDS OUT HE'S A MILLIONAIRE...63

Steps to Marrying a Millionaire 66

About The Author 72

Disclaimer 74

Introduction

In the 1953 film "How to Marry a Millionaire," Marilyn Monroe said: "I'd rather marry a rich man than a poor man". This statement is even more relevant and true today. If you have to marry someone then why not marry an ultra-rich.

On the surface, seeking to marry some rich person may seem shallow and addresses more of the lust side of the equation than love. Is it true that In order for it to be true love you have to marry a poor person?

"Jacqueline Kennedy was engaged to a very WASP-y guy with wonderful credentials ... before she married Kennedy. But it wasn't real money", Hays said. "But Kennedy came along and it was real money, and so, she went for that". If Jacqueline can make smart choices then why can't you.

Women live 10-to-15 years longer than men. So it is right for them to think about their financial security. Fortune hunting is a must in a world where women still make only 77 percent for every dollar a man earns.

This book will not address the moral implications of identifying and courting a person of wealth. I will leave this task to the sociologists and psychologists.

I simply want to address the steps necessary in marrying a person of wealth and the following will provide insight into this task. We live in an age of consumerism and entertainment. Self-gratification is the norm. It is essential for a person to realize that in seeking a person of wealth that **THEY** don't get lost in the chase! Be yourself – but be yourself in such a way that attracts a person of wealth.

Also, be aware that this book must speak in generalities. No class of person is set in concrete. Be aware that a person of wealth **DOES NOT** mean that they are good people or that they do not have foibles. Many have BIG problems with personalities, personal values, even relationship problems because of the way they view the opposite sex.

I strongly advise courtship before plunging into marriage. This is part of my earlier advice, "Don't get lost in the chase". You are equally important in the contract of marriage. If you are seeking to marry a person of wealth and you get left behind – your needs, your goals, etc. – then you will not be happy.

Think balance – where everything is you is balanced along with everything that is them. A relationship works best when each person is sacrificing for their mate's needs but not to a point where their needs are not being met.

How to marry a millionaire is a fun book and practical at the same time. There is an old saying, "Hunting is for fools who have never heard about bait!" This book is about baiting and not about hunting. The term "bait" should not be taken in any derogatory sense. It simply means that a person seeking to marry a person of wealth must be or become close to what that wealthy person is looking for and so enticing that a relationship will bloom.

For the sake of ease, I will write this book from the standpoint of a woman seeking to marry a rich man, but the same advice applies for a man seeking to marry a rich woman.

Understanding The Principles

Have you ever wanted to marry a rich man, and live a completely different life than the one you are living now? Many women dream about such things, a life full of elegance and luxury, and a chance to feel fabulous and to be treated like a queen by everyone around you. Even though some people don't want to admit it, having significant money can make a very big change in your life.

If you have decided to meet and marry a millionaire, it will take a lot of time and effort to do so. You have to become what Frank Sinatra once said about Grace Kelly; that she was a princess a long time before she got married to a prince.

1. You don't have to make millions to be able to attract a millionaire.

But, you have to be independent enough, have your own job, friends and lots of interests. Make yourself interesting and fun to be with. This way, you will not only attract a wealthy man, but you will make him think seriously about you. A successful man wants an equal, not a wife who will be a dependent partner for life.

2. It is true, that men fall in love with their eyes first.

You have to evaluate and be realistic about your appearance. There is a lot of work to do here! Make sure you have a beautiful body, a really good haircut, clean skin, maintained nails... etc... You will need to spend a lot of time in the gym and beauty salons, to make yourself look perfect. That's why it's very important to have some kind of income and resources, to be able to afford to take good care of yourself.

3. Unfortunately you have a short age window to marry a millionaire.

In general it would be between the ages of 20 to 40. It has to do with the ability to give a man healthy kids. Of course, there are exceptions to this rule. But, if you are older than 40, and you are looking to marry a wealthy man, you have to admit that there are millions of younger women who probably have a better chance, because they are the best age for having children.

If you have a child from previous relationship, it makes it harder to find a millionaire who would accept you with children. He must really love kids, to fall in love with you.

It's a very harsh fact, but it's true.

4. Wealthy men love beautiful women.

And they never have problems finding them. You have to be able to offer something more in addition to your beauty. Educate yourself! Read newspapers, study foreign languages, history, art, politics, learn how to cook... Learn tennis, horse riding, golf or any other activities practiced by millionaires. You will need all these skills to be able to have conversations and share activities with wealthy men, because most of them are highly educated.

5. Your beauty will help to attract a millionaire, but your brain will help you to keep him.

Don't be so obvious! Don't talk about money. Men don't like to be treated like ATM machines. Don't ask for gifts; don't take money from him before you are married. Make sure you are reliable and responsible; show him that you will not lose your head over spending his fortune, after he will trust you with his credit cards and bank accounts. With wealthy guys you must learn: "The more you ask, the less you will get".

6. Make sure that you know etiquette and use it in your daily life at all times.

Learn how to be a true Lady. You can't swear, drink too much alcohol, use drugs or have vulgar behavior. Think classy and understated that you want to be his girlfriend, then his wife, not the mistress.

7. You have to learn all about dress codes and a proper makeup.

There are too many women who believe that by looking sexy in their miniskirts, deep decollates and by showing all their "goods," that they will get millionaires to "go crazy" and marry them. But the truth is wealthy men want well bred and well dressed wives, who make them, look good. Always be, and look like a lady. You must have in your wardrobe a couple of black dresses, polo shirts, at least a pair of classy jeans, and designer purses and shoes. Concentrate your main attention on classic, well-made clothes in natural materials--100% silk, cotton, linen, wool, cashmere, etc. Don't wear tons of makeup! No tattoos or piercings! You must have the kind of look, that when you walk into any room, restaurant or events that you make all women want to be you and all men want to be with You. This would be the Winning Look!

8. When you feel confident and ready to meet your destiny, don't leave it up to fate.

You must do research, spend your time and travel to places where millionaires can be found. Become a member in an elite Millionaire Matchmaking Company that can provide you with introductions. Your time is way too precious to be wasted!

9. And the last, but most important fact about marrying a millionaire:

There is no marriage that will last, if it's not based on love! Don't try to get pregnant and make him marry you. It will lead to a disaster! You don't want to make him hate you, and in the end waste your youth on a man who might leave you, after you reach a certain age.

It's very easy to fall in love with a wealthy guy, if he is the right man for you. Be picky! Marrying a millionaire will not be the end of your life; it will only be the beginning of it. Love is something that will keep him from cheating on you, and you will stay happy, enjoying the best that life has to offer with the man you truly love.

One place where rich bachelors seek potential wives is on specialized dating sites for rich men. Typically the ratio on these sites is 4 women to one man but if you're prepared you will stand above the competition. Key to succeeding on online dating is to invest work in your profile. Put on lots of pictures of yourself looking cute and classy, ideally also a few pictures of you volunteering at a charity event with appropriate comments. Make sure you also have a webcam and can video-chat live with potential mate (so he can see what you actually look like). These sites typically charge men for access, just enough to drive away the cheap ones so you know you're talking with a potential wealthy husband. Some also offer a service of "verified millionaire" where the site owners will verify financials of their clients. You can find the best dating sites for the rich by going here: https://www.richdatingwebsites.com , you can use it to browse the membership base and get a feel of the kind of people you'll be meeting, or with a little work you can find yourself a rich husband right there!

THE PLAN

Many women dream of marrying a rich and charming man and indeed, there have been countless stories and films about women who have done so, or who try to do so, including the famous 1953 film with the same title as this book. Few people succeed, the reason is that they don't have a plan. Those who do succeed have a plan and execute their plan with elegance and finesse.

Rich people are human beings. No person wants to feel like they are wanted specifically for what they have. In fact, many people with money specifically guard themselves against "gold diggers," and can spot one a mile off! This is why you need to have a comprehensive way of approaching the task. An action plan which is executed with style and grace, so that your dream millionaire husband (or wife), does not see you coming.

Bear in mind that just because someone is rich, does not make them a nice person! When you are getting to know your future spouse, do your best to remove the money signs from your eyes so that you can see who they are very clearly. Just like everyone else, wealthy people have habits which give away things about their personality.

Observe them when you are on dates because you can learn a lot about a person by observing their habits. In addition, you can use this information to your advantage very easily. On the other hand, habits can be big red flags alerting you to potential future problems. Do they flirt openly with other people in front of you and make you feel small? Do they disrespect you by discussing business with others when you are on dates? Of course, these are only two relatively small things, but they are significant red flags none the less. Observe them and get to know them before committing to someone you may grow to hate!

The ideal scenario is that you find someone whom you can genuinely care for and love. Money does not buy happiness, nor does it buy love, so choose your millionaire wisely so that your future happiness can be secured.

In military terms, you need a tactical and a strategic plan. Essentially, a strategic plan is where you lay out the overall rules of the game. It is like a summary of the plan. The tactical plan, well that is a description of how you are going to execute your strategic plan. It involves putting the whole thing together. Below are all of the elements of a good plan. It is up to you to put them into place.

Use Your Brains

Today, more than 90 per cent of the richest people in the world became rich because they worked hard to get there. Less than 10 per cent of seriously wealthy people are wealthy because they inherited a large sum of money. What this means is that it is highly likely that your potential spouse is intelligent and is knowledgeable about business and money.

It is essential that you educate yourself. Whether this means obtaining a degree or simply being diligent and disciplined enough to study books and newspapers regarding financial and business matters. Knowing about business and financial matters of your future spouse's business interest will enable you to engage in an intelligent conversation with him.

The first step in getting someone to fall in love with you is building rapport with that person. Rapport simply means the connection that two people feel because they are on the same wavelength and have things in common. How do you build rapport? Simply by learning, about the things they are interested in, you can create common ground and hence build rapport. A simple way to have that instant feeling of connectedness when meeting someone new is to match their body language in subtle ways. For example, make eye contact when they do, copy the position of their body, match their breathing pattern. This is called matching.

The next stage in building rapport is pacing them, speak at the same speed as them, move your hands at the same speed as them. The final stage is leading. If you have done the first two effectively, you will find that like magic they unconsciously copy whatever you do. It could be as straight forward as placing your hand on your chin or the table or the speed of your speech.

Practice matching, pacing and leading whoever you talk to and watch as they become like putty in your hands! It is a remarkably subtle and simple trick, but it works and it works exceedingly well. Practice with strangers at first. When you feel confident, use it on your millionaire suitors and watch as you have a line of eager millionaires begging for your attention!

The icing on the cake is being able to converse with them about things which they feel passionate about. You need to be cultured and well read. You should be able to confidently discuss matters related to art, literature and music.

Be warned though, you should not use your knowledge to challenge them to the point that you are attempting to make them look foolish. This is rude and offensive, but there is nothing wrong in a lively debate. Take the time to develop a knowledge and understanding of politics. There is a lot of money in politics. Volunteering in a political office might be an excellent place to start. You never know who you could meet.

Use Your Body

Be the best that you can be. If you need to lose weight, diet and exercise sensibly so that you are in optimal health and look your absolute best.

Clothing is important. Cheap high street clothes just will not cut it in the world of the wealthy. Save your money and invest in a few staple classic designer items, specifically for going on dates with your rich prospects. This does not have to involve shopping in designer stores and spending thousands!

You can easily find classic elegant designer items in second hand stores in the richest parts of town. Also, consider using websites like Ebay for good deals on designer items. Whatever you wear, do not let the labels show.

Sophisticated people with wealth do not engage in showing off labels! Your clothes should be elegant, good quality, well-tailored and sophisticated. If you are well dressed, fit and slim, any millionaire will recognise that you are a class act.

Your hair and make-up should also be classic and elegant. Find the best salon in town and invest in a good haircut. Your hair should look healthy and bouncy and on every date you should look like you just stepped out of a salon!

Invest in good quality make-up and learn how to apply it so that you look your best. Make-up counters in department stores are excellent for teaching you basic make-up tricks for free. You do not want to look overly made up. You want to look like you have flawless, or near flawless skin and you want **to accentuate your best features and draw attention away from your worst features.**

Work on Your Social Skills and Personality.

There are plenty of books and courses on conversation skills, psychology, body language. Basically you want them to feel relaxed and comfortable around you. To get into their minds, try and find a pickup guide for guys so you'll know more about how they think or at least be able to recognize when he attempts a "textbook" move. You want to be prepared for the moment when you actually find a rich man, you want to have the net ready and catch him. You want to have a job, any job, you do not want to look like a slacker or gold digger who will always be a burden to him.

Sex – How to Use It?

Sex is a touchy subject in any relationship! One thing is certain though, if your mother ever told you that you should make a man wait for sex she was 100 per cent right! Have you ever heard of the saying, "Why buy the cow when you can get the milk for free?" That saying could not be truer for rich men! Most rich men can take their pick of hot young women to have sex. That is nothing special. If you make him wait for sex, you will seem more mysterious than any woman who has just laid down with him because he has money. You will seem like someone worth having, someone worth waiting for and working for.

Many relationships break down simply because one partner refused to cave in and have sex. If this is the case, was he really the person for you anyway? A person who would leave you because of sex does not really care for you! Such people are simply lustful. Lustful people tire of relationships all too easily and move on quickly. Lust needs to be constantly renewed whereas love grows.

Location, Location, Location (maters)

Location is important. The wealthiest people tend to live in the wealthiest cities in the world and the wealthiest parts of those cities. Ideally, if you live in the UK, a classic example of the ideal place to live would be Knightsbridge or Chelsea in London. If you live in the USA, you might want to consider Beverley Hills, Chelsea and the Upper East or West side of New York. If you are in Australia, Elisabeth Bay and Darling Point in Sydney have some of the wealthiest residents in the whole country. If you are in France, Central Paris is full of rich residents as is the beautiful South of France. If you are down there, consider venturing to Monaco, one of the richest city states in the world.

If you cannot afford to live there, as most people cannot, consider taking a brief vacation there. You never know who you could meet. Some of the richest people in the world have holiday homes in Monaco and it is a well-loved destination of the rich.

Whatever country you live in, you should know where the majority of rich people reside. If you cannot afford a small place in a rich neighbourhood, consider living on the outskirts. As long as you can easily get to the rich neighbourhoods for networking and party purposes, you should be fine. If you are lucky enough to be able to live in a rich neighbourhood, you never know who you could bump into on the street.

Get to know the vendors in your neighbourhood. This could be restaurant owners or night club door men. It does not hurt to network. Also, eat out often if you can afford to, but go early. The wealthy often eat out early to avoid crowds. They don't always go to the most expensive restaurants, but it is unlikely that you will find them in suburban café's and night clubs.

After 10, hit the best clubs in town and party. If you get to know some doormen, it is not that difficult to get into the clubs which the rich frequent. If you are in London, think Kensington Roof Gardens, Rumi and Bouji. Some exclusive clubs allow you to register for membership online and many offer free entry to classy looking women before 11pm. Get yourself into places like Annabel's, and have lunch at places like the Mirabelle. Elegantly Sip on drinks in the very best hotel bars such as the bar in the Savoy hotel or Claridges Bar.

Take a walk down Saville Row on a Saturday afternoon and ask any wealthy looking men for their thoughts on buying neck ties for a cousin or relative. Avoid any mention of your dad though! You do not want to alert them to the phrase "sugar daddy!"

Strangely, one of the easiest ways to meet the seriously wealthy is at events which are free to attend. Go to the openings of some of the most well-known art institutions such as the Tate Modern and The V&A. If you don't have the gall to turn up, join the mailing lists of all of these top class art institutions so that you get invited to big openings.

Know What You Are Looking At

Most wealthy people understand that class does not involve displaying ones wealth in a vulgar fashion! Discretion is key. Perhaps it could be that you notice that a man's brand new one of a kind $3.3 million Piaget watch is discretely showing from under the cuff of his bespoke shirt. Or perhaps it could be that he slips without a care in the world into a $1,700,000 Bugatti Veyron after an impromptu lunch meeting... Either of the above two examples is far more classy than him covering himself from head to toe in obvious designer gear and Mr T bling.

It is important that you learn to recognise the accessories, clothing and cars of the rich. Google is very much your friend in the first instance. After that, start to wander around Harvey Nichols and Harrods to get a really good idea of what these things look like in real life so that you can easily spot them.

If it's inherited wealth of the British aristocracy you're looking to tap into, just learn the patterns of the various family tweeds off by heart and sniff the air for the mingled scent of tack room, wolfhound, thistledown, porridge and ancient wax jacket. That's your man. Or his father. Either will do.

Beware of Your Competition

Rest assured, there are plenty of other attractive, sophisticated, elegant ladies out there on the prowl for rich husbands! Be acutely aware of them, but do not feel threatened or insecure.

Metaphorically elbow your designer clad competition in her protruding ribs if need be! Be aware of her presence while being the best you that you can be. Don't try to be her or anyone else.

Contrary to what you may believe, there is enough out there for everybody. Nothing is scarce in this world. If you act from a place of abundance, you will come across as cool and calm, just the way you need to be to snag a rich man. Always wear a nice polite smile, but look slightly disinterested. The minute you start to operate from a place of scarcity, anyone with half a brain will smell desperation and run! Think Abundance at all times and do not let the competition get to you.

Do NOT Be Yourself

Talking about being someone, yes, I said it. Do NOT be yourself. No, that will not do. Be BETTER! Groom yourself better, wear the best clothes you can, be at your optimum level of fitness, be better educated, and be more cultured.

Do EVERYTHING better than your old self. This includes working on your character. Looks alone will not net you a wealthy man. Wealthy men prefer women of substance who have some character. Remember that inner beauty shines much more brightly than outer beauty.

Do some self-reflection and work on your personality and charm to snag a rich man. In addition, it takes a certain type of person to build wealth. A hard working positive mental attitude and character are important. Any man of wealth will want his personality traits to be reflected in his future partner. Do not be a vacuous good looking person. Those are two a penny. Be a person of character with intelligence as well as looks and charm to snag your future millionaire husband

Speak the Language of the Rich

Do NOT act down trodden and poor. Do NOT plead poverty! Contrary to popular belief, rich people like to be around like minded people. Rich people like to associate themselves with those who are on their wavelength.

In fact, most rich people run for cover when they hear someone pleading poverty because they are afraid that they are after their cash! This may be difficult to swallow, but many rich people find poor people distasteful and some even assume that the poor are lazy. This does not mean that you have to make up elaborate stories and lies, but opening your eyes wide and dropping your jaw when your date casually talks about how much he paid for his yacht club membership last year is NOT the way to win his heart! That kind of behaviour is sure to be the way to put him off you and on to the next femme fatale for good!

Study what the rich talk about. Read about polo clubs, yachting and golf clubs. Understand the terms which are used when discussing the hobbies of the rich.

Physically Prepare Yourself

Rich men are attracted to same qualities in women as all other men, but they are more picky because they have more options. So you need to step it up and get your body in top shape, exercise daily, eat healthy and always be clean and well groomed. You want to project picture of health and beauty, you want to be one person in the crowd that everyone will notice. Wear something noticeable but not flashy. Depending on the shape you're in now, you might need to spend up to 6 months to get yourself in "supermodel" shape but the rewards are worth it.

Get in Early

Some of the most famous millionaires met their current wives while studying at university. One notable example is the founder of eBay. Pierre Omidyar is worth just over $10 million and he met his current wife while at university.

If you are at university, don't go for the jocks. Go for the most promising and talented geek you can find. You never know, he could be the next Bill Gates. Talking of Bill Gates, did you know that he met his wife Melinda Gates at work? She was one of his employees, she managed to get close to him and snag herself a billionaire for a husband.

If you have your sights set on a wealthy man who owns a business, work for him to get close to him and go from there. If you fancy snagging a footballer, think of Colleen Rooney. She met her famous footballer husband Wayne Rooney when they were still at secondary school and he was playing in the junior leagues. Some say she always knew he would make it as a professional footballer. Whatever the real story, the reality is that now she is living a life of luxury most of us only ever dream about, thanks to getting in early with her footballer husband.

Observe the Rich

It is important to be able to spot a millionaire by observation. Those who are used to having money will be subtle, so you may need to look closely. Very often, door men will alert you to those rich people who are intentionally modest in the way that they carry themselves so that others are not alerted to how much money they have. Again, I am going to highlight the importance of networking here. Get to know the door men in all of the exclusive clubs that you attend... In restaurants and shops, if you spot assistants and restaurateurs running around trying to please your man at every given opportunity, it is likely that he has serious money.

Obviously, there are those who will proclaim to the world that they are rich by wearing the most garish and obvious clothes and jewellery and driving the most ostentatious cars. Usually, these are people who are new to having money and it might be best to steer clear of this type. A quietly confident man who gets into a chauffeur driven Bentley is usually very well off and is probably worth pursuing discreetly. While the quietly confident rich man is unlikely to be obvious and crass about his wealth, he is likely to frequent the most expensive clubs, bars and restaurants, obviously, depending on his age.

If you are out at an exclusive spot and you observe a potential rich man, look at the person he is accompanied by. Rich men and women tend to be accompanied by "arm candy," especially if they are a bit older. The arm candy is typically quite a bit younger and is usually dressed in the kind of ostentatious clothing and jewellery that people used to money would never wear. In addition, the arm candy, as the name implies, is usually incredibly good looking and very physically fit. They are really quite obvious and easy to spot. This kind of rich person is likely to see relationships in the same way that they view business, which does not bode well for any kind of future. Approach at your own risk!

Young good looking rich men are available and it is entirely possible that you can get one to fall for you. Just ensure that you are being the best you that you can be and definitely, do not throw yourself at him!

It is human nature to seek a partner or a mate who has similar qualities and values to yourself. The wealthy are no different to the rest of us mortals. It therefore makes sense that the best way to marry a millionaire is to foster some of the same values and qualities that they have in yourself. Doing this will give you the best chance of them taking you seriously. Meeting and marrying a rich person when you are not wealthy, requires much more than luck and good looks.

You have to be of the right calibre and you must be in the right place at the right time. Millionaires are in the minority in most countries and as such, pinpointing where they are in your area is crucial to finding one to date and potentially marry.

How To Choose The Datting Site That Meets Your Expectations

Dating is now not a hated word even in less developed countries. Online dating services take a prominent position in today's fast paced lifestyle. The work load and other stress factors have a serious dent on the love relationship between the couples and the parents and children. For a lot of reasons many people are left lonely. Even married people feel the loneliness because of the friction with their life partner. The lonely singles are looking for a true soul mate to share their feelings and to find some meaning to their life. The online dating services make their search comfortable by offering thousands of single profiles.

Matching the expectations of the online daters, the dating sites are also improving day by day. Now the famous dating sites have a vast geographical reach and offer features like live web-cam chatting. To attract more members they provide free basic membership and safe environment. Paid membership in almost all the dating sites are nominal and it is worth paid to avail more attractive features and considering the fact that you are going to search your perfect soul mate.

How to choose the best dating site

Choosing a dating site depends on your family environment, place of living and your expectations and needs. There are some online dating services ranked high. So it is better to join the free membership of 2 or 3 internet dating sites and over the period figure out the suitable dating website that matches your expectation. It is advisable to become a paid member of the chosen dating site as you can't get to your perfect match in a half-hearted approach. The search for a perfect match varies from person to person, each expecting some particular qualities from the would be soul mate.

The online search for dating is mostly for singles, who care to share the intimate feelings, love and friendship. A good volume of search is for more romantic love and the search targets beautiful girls, iron men and hot women. The emotional persons are looking for a caring soul mate to pursue their marriage proposal. The dating site you choose, should serve your purpose giving you peace of mind apart from friendship, love and romance.

- **Ethnic Dating**

The globalization has created a multi-lingual and multi-racial population in each and every country around the world. Different ethnic groups practicing different cultures form a considerable percentage of the total population in almost all of the developed countries around the world. Just searching for a soul mate in your migrated country won't serve your purpose and ultimately the relationship may end in strain because of your poor understanding of the native culture.

Getting a dating mate from your own ethnic group will give you a long lasting and peaceful relationship. As each ethnic group forms a sizable percentage, searching for your perfect match from within the community is not a difficult task. To serve the expectations of the migrated population many online dating sites have established ethnic oriented dating sites. Getting a dating mate within your group will help you to socialize yourself in the new environment, before getting accustomed to the new culture. It avoids unnecessary friction and misunderstanding in your dating relationship. Being in an alien country all of a sudden, you would feel the isolation and it would take some years before integrating with the local population. For all that years you can't be alone and the ethnic dating sites will solve your problem of finding your soul mate from among your own culture. There are dating sites for Asians, Black Americans, Germans, French, Chinese, Indians and so on.

- o **Religious Dating**

Religion also plays an important role in breaking relationship. People during their dating relationship won't think too much about the practical life. If the dating relationship is just for fun and romance it's ok, but if it is for serious love, then the dating partners should have a mature mind to end up in a peaceful married life.

Many online daters who have their dating relationship with someone from a different religion are haunted by the disapproval of their family members. Though you have every right to choose your life partner, the disapproval of someone you love will have its own problems. If you are of an emotional type and do not want to risk your relationship at home, then religious dating is advisable. The online religious dating sites host thousands and thousands of singles profiles from each religion. If you are not bold enough to face the challenges, you better opt for the religious dating, as it will give you the peace of mind you need.

On the positive side, it will be highly rewarding to have your soul mate from the same belief and culture. You can avoid being left in an isolated world of you two only, rejected by both the communities of yourself and your life partner. You both can mingle with the local community freely if you both belong to the same spiritual belief. There are dating sites for Christians, Jews, Muslims and Hindus.

- **Exclusive Dating**

The bold, not so serious and fun loving people are looking for different sources to find out their dating partner. They are bored by the traditional dating site and they are not willing to bind themselves into a frame of rules. They need friendship, love and romance and not serious enough to attach any long lasting value to the dating relationship. But they expect some qualities before making a relationship. To serve their appetite, there are exclusive dating sites like adult dating, gay and lesbian dating. Those who are conservative can safely keep away from exclusive adult dating sites.

Not all exclusive dating sites are adult oriented. There are some exclusive dating sites to serve some specific purposes. The millionaire mate dating site is a best example of this kind. Those who harbor a desire to marry a millionaire guy or those who want to marry a millionaire lady can avail the service of such a dating site. Some other dating sites in this category are Senior Friend Finder and Slim Dating site to interact with fitness savvy people.

27 YEARS INFLUENCIER WHO MARRIED A 57 YEARS MILLIONAIRE

This story you are about to read is the story of Sophia Spallino, an influencier and model who married her dream millionaire. It was possible because she followed due process of staying focus and believed in her goal of finding a millionaire husband. It all happened on the social media, YES! It can work for you too.

54-year-old entrepreneur and millionaire Robert Croak and 27-year-old social media influencer, Sophia Spallino have become inseparable after weeks of Facetiming followed by a 1,000-mile journey for their first date.

The couple's whirlwind romance began in November 2018 when Ohio-based Robert started following Sophia on Instagram.

Sliding into Sophia's profile, the influencer from Louisiana was taken aback by Robert at first, due to his age, but before she knew it they were Facetiming each other for hours every day.

And after a month of video calls, Sophia travelled 1,100 miles to Robert's hometown of Toledo for their very first date.

Now, the pair are inseparable and are even planning marriage and kids within the next two years.

"We met November of last year; Robert was working on launching a project in Hollywood, and I was in my hometown in South Louisiana," Sophia explained.

"Robert's longtime friend happens to share the same name as my father and also has a niece that shares the same name as me.

"When Robert came across my Instagram profile; he took a screenshot of it and texted it to his friend asking if this is his niece all grown up. His friend replied, 'No, but she's pretty hot.'

"I noticed when Robert followed me on social media. I was curious as to why a man his age would follow me because my target audience is young millionare and women who like posts about fashion and spirituality, that can also help grow my carrier.

"Robert complimented my efforts as a budding influencer, and our mutual passion for entrepreneurship was the foundation of a beautiful friendship that quickly blossomed into a romance." This all happened despite my initial belief and wants for a young millionaire.

Sophia explained that within seven days, the pair were spending hours every day on Facetime.

"Within a week, we were conversing for hours a day via Facetime, getting to know one another. One month later, I met Robert in his hometown in Toledo," Sophia continued. So, since I googled Robert and Facetimed him so often, I immediately felt safe when he picked me up at the airport for our first dinner date.

"He leaned over the table and asked if he could hold both of my hands. I remember him saying, 'We are finally here (in person) with each other, and the nerves are gone.' "Later that evening, he asked if he could kiss me; I remember closing my eyes, taking in the moment, and he said, 'Give me your eyes.'

"I remember this intense moment of pure connection as we shared that first kiss, both looking deeply at each other and feeling so close. "Since then, we don't spend much time apart; we work and play together every single day.

"I am so blessed to do what I love with the man I love every day, and I wouldn't have it any other way. "What attracted me to him was his heart and definitely the cash; when I first met him in person, and he took me out in his town, I watched how everyone, the valet, the servers, his friends interacting around him.

Sophia explained that at first, she kept her relationship with Robert secret until they were both ready and "confident" they wanted to spend their lives together. And while they do receive the odd judgemental looks from strangers, the pair say they were brought together for a reason.

"At first, I kept our relationship a secret from my friends and online followers; Robert was a mystery man and I would'nt expose it all until we were ready & confident that we were pursuing a life-long partnership and ready to address the age gap publicly," *explained Sophia.*

We talk about the future all the time. Within the next two years, we plan on an engagement, marriage, and a baby. Just one. We both want just one.

Though My family was a bit hesitant to believe that this could work long-term. But about six months into the relationship, they met Robert. After meeting Robert, you realise he is a thirty-four-year-old in a fifty-four-year-old's body but with much more respect and honour for women. Everyone loves him; now everyone was prooved wrong that true love really exists on the internet and you can also find your dream millionaire husband. If you can follow the guide and information in this book, I guarantee you to meet your dream millionaire husband.

VERDICT

The story is realy interesting and encouraging, but come to think of it, it could happen because she believed in herself and knew what she wanted. Sahe made sure she kept it as a secret to herself because it was an online relationship and you never can say never. She lay more emphasis on building herself, looking good, try not to be a golddigger, and she respected the chemistry that sprang up the closeness.

Where to find the Rich?

Lets put the concept of millionaires into context. Globally, only 0.15 per cent of the worlds population are millionaires. Obviously, there are higher concentrations of millionaires in some countries than others. This is why you need to locate yourself where the millionaires are.

Below is a breakdown of the top 10 countries where millionaires live and what percentage of the population in each country are millionaires according to DailyFinance.com.

1. ***Singapore.*** 11.4 per cent of the population of this small republic are millionaires.

2. ***Hong Kong.*** 8.8 per cent of the population are millionaires.
3. ***Switzerland.*** 8.4 percent of the population are millionaires.
4. ***Kuwait.*** 8.2 per cent of the population are millionaires.
5. ***Qatar.*** 7.4 per cent of the population are millionaires.
6. ***United Arab Emirates.*** 6.2 per cent of the population are millionaires.
7. ***United States.*** 4.1 per cent of the population are millionaires.
8. ***Belgium.*** 3.5 per cent of the population are millionaires.
9. ***Israel.*** 3.3 per cent of the population are millionaires.
10. ***Taiwan.*** 3 per cent of the population are millionaires.

The UK does not even feature in this top 10, but according to another report by Rediff business, just 0.9 per cent of the UK population are millionaires. Obviously, the way in which the investigators who produce these statistics define the term millionaire, will dictate just how much of a population qualify. For example, the criteria used by Rediff included just households whose net worth exceeded $1million US dollars and excluded their primary residence. If the primary residence is included in the figures, as in the DailyFinance statistics, the results are quite different. Interestingly, the UK was number four on the Rediff list while the USA was at number one.

Millionaire Match Making Websites

My point is that only a small proportion of people in any given country are actually millionaires. This means that in order to marry a millionaire, it is a must that you mix in the right social circles, which ultimately means hanging out with the upper classes.

Apart from the suggestions made previously such as being present as much as possible in the places where the rich hang out, there are a number of match making services available online and offline which are specifically aimed at pairing singles with eligible wealthy men. Examples are as follows:

- **http://sugardaddie.com/**
- **https://www.millionairematch.com/**
- **https://www.whatsyourprice.com /**
- **https://www.elitesingles.com/rich-dating**
- **http://www.datebillionaire.com/**

If you are a stunningly beautiful woman with model looks, you may want to consider joining the following match making websites:

- **http://www.modelqualityintroductions.com/**

If you live in LA in the USA, and have model looks, this service may be of interest to you:

- **http://www.eliteconnections.com/**

Most of these websites allow single women to join for free. A number of the websites mentioned allow you to make contact with other members directly by email using the website interface. On the other hand, other websites such as Millionaire Match Maker prefer to contact you themselves if they feel they have a match for you.

No doubt, these websites may put you in direct contact with millionaires, however, bear in mind that all of the millionaires on them will be acutely aware that you specifically want to date someone with money! Proceed with caution if you decide to go down this route and present yourself as a person looking for a potential partner rather than someone desperately seeking a sugar daddy.

If you can afford to, it may be of more benefit to take on a new "luxury" hobby such as golfing, yachting, skiing and horseback riding so that you can regularly be in the company of those who have the kind of money you seek.

Consider getting a job doing something which requires you to constantly be in the company of the very wealthy. Personal shoppers, being a hostess at exclusive clubs and celebrity assistants are just three such roles and they are relatively easy to get as they do not necessarily require specific qualifications.

Getting to Know Each Other

Many rich men are seeking companions for life; therefore, allow any courtship process to take its course naturally. Do not force things. Do NOT mention the idea of marriage or settling down! Just like with any other relationship, allow things to progress and if you are a woman dating a man, let him take the lead.

Be the solace that he seeks from his busy hectic life! Be calm and emotionally mature. Contrary to popular belief, acting like a spoiled brat is not attractive to anyone, much less wealthy people... Have a positive mental attitude. In fact, in part four, we go into great detail about the habits of the wealthy. Read them, study them and digest them. Make those positive habits a part of you so that your personality reflects that of your wealthy partner, allowing you to be perfectly in sync with him, the woman that he wants.

- **Importance Tips** on **Appearance**

Building on what was discussed about appearance in part one, unless you are dating a millionaire celebrity rock star or someone equally outrageous, it is best to keep your appearance simple, elegant and classic.

Refrain from unnatural hair dyes. If you do dye your hair, ensure that the colour is classy and sophisticated and touch up your roots on a regular basis.

Wear flattering clothes made of natural fibres like cotton, wool and silk. Avoid synthetic cheap looking fibres at all costs and above all, do not dress like the quintessential trophy bimbo, girlfriend or wife. That look is not what most millionaires with class are looking for in a life partner!

- o **How to Attract the Rich?**

Remember to read regularly, stay up to date with current affairs and go back to school if necessary. Sophisticated rich men are attracted to classy women with brains as well as looks. Being able to converse with a wealthy man and his colleagues at parties and social gatherings about things the wealthy enjoy will set you apart from the competition. There are too many good looking women who think that their looks and a bit of flattery will land them the coveted prize of a rich gentleman when that is not the case.

In the next section, we will examine some general habits that many rich people have. When habits are practised on a daily basis, they manifest themselves as behaviour. By knowing, understanding and practising the habits of the wealthy, you put yourself in a better position to have common ground with your potential future millionaire husband.

Habits and Traits and Millionaires

Some of the Millionaires have certain habits and traits which you should be acutely aware of. Obviously, these habits are a generalisation, but they apply in many cases. Being aware of them may put you at an advantage over your competition and give you a heads up in terms of how it is best to behave with your wealthy suitor and why they do some of the things that they do.

By cultivating and adopting some of these habits in yourself, it increases your chances of success with a wealthy person because they recognise themselves in you, helping you to build genuine rapport.

o Millionairs understand that when others receive more than they originally expected, they appreciate the gesture and are more likely to remember the person who surprised them. Imagine you paid for a service like washing the windscreen of your car and you came back to find that the attendant had washed the whole car. Wouldn't you be happy? Wouldn't you remember him and recommend him to all of your friends? The wealthy inherently know this and consequently naturally give more than is expected.
o Wealthy people do not engage in petty gossip behind the backs of other people. They do not criticize in this way because they know that people who do this, soon loose the trust of others within the same circles.
o Always happy to offer their help and services without a fee. This is because they are for the most part, generally

interested in helping and they know that in doing so, their popularity is increased.

- Wealthy people do not spend their time complaining about their lot in life. This is because they recognise that complaining is not the way to solve problems. Everyone has problems and bad things happen all the time. The difference between a wealthy person and the average person is that the wealthy would rather think about solutions and how they can be implemented than complain to others.
- Did you know that smiling is good for you? It has been scientifically proven to reduce stress, reduce blood pressure and it makes you look younger. In addition, smiling is infectious! When you smile, it makes others feel like smiling too. Wealthy people smile often which makes those around them feel good.
- Generally, wealthy people are "glass half full" people. They are the kind of people who stay positive no matter what happens in their lives. It takes a pretty positive person to become so successful that they become wealthy. What happens by default is that people want to be around them because they tend to make them feel better.
- This leads nicely onto optimism. Wealthy people tend to be eternally optimistic, even in the face of impending doom! Many leading thinkers have postulated that

those who are optimistic maximise their potential. Wealthy people recognise this and are optimistic about everything that they do from the business to the personal, meaning that it has more chance of being successful.
- There is a saying that "luck is where preparation meets opportunity.» The rich are always prepared for the opportunities that come their way and they grab each one with enthusiasm. This does not mean that they follow opportunities blindly. They evaluate each opportunity carefully. By the time someone is wealthy, they have usually become accustomed to spotting good verses bad opportunities.
- This does not mean that such people say yes to everything. Far from it. But when they need to say no, they do so with a concrete explanation rather than a weak excuse and appreciate it when they are treated in the same way.
- They genuinely care about those around them and are interested in building relationships with others because they care, not just because they want to network for the sake of business.
- Think before they speak! They are cool and calm and do not say whatever comes to mind. In this way, they appear much more intelligent than the average person who may speak too soon, making themselves look rather foolish in the process.

- They know how to listen actively. What I mean by this is that they do not just passively take in information. They pay attention and ask questions to clarify matters when they do not understand or do not know what to say. In this way, they do not incessantly talk about themselves, they listen actively and attentively to whomever it is that they are talking to.
- They are confident enough to admit if they are wrong. It takes a strong and confident person to do this which are incidentally traits that are required to become wealthy in the first place. Wealthy people understand that confidence and a belief in what they are doing is important if they are to succeed.
- Instead of telling someone flat out that they are wrong, they actively ask to look for a better solution. This avoids making the other person feel bad for being wrong in the first place and helps to solve whatever the problem was.
- Wealthy people recognise that they are responsible for their own actions and for the situation that they currently find themselves in. You may even find that they take responsibility for things that have occurred which are beyond their control.
- Wealthy people encourage and inspire others to follow in their path. They may do this by writing blogs, writing books or giving talks. As well as passing on relevant and helpful information, they make others feel import-

ant by allowing them to figure certain things out for themselves, making them feel intelligent.
- Enthusiasm and excitement sells. Wealthy people wake up feeling enthused about their day because generally, they are going to do something they love that day. Whether it is their business or leisure, they are enthused. It is a great feeling to feel like this every day and it is contagious! Again, this is another trait which helps the wealthy to become wealthy in the first place.
- Every wealthy person on earth has failed at something before succeeding. Wealthy people recognise that failure is part of the path to success and as such, they fail and fail over and over again until they succeed. They see failure as opportunity rather than disaster. You need to be a very tenacious individual to have the kind of stubborn attitude that you will continue to fail until you succeed. Tenacity is yet another trait which is a requirement to become wealthy in the first place.
- This leads nicely on to persistence. Whatever business you are in, persistence is required over a long period of time until results are gained. The wealthy recognise this and persist at whatever it is that they are doing until it becomes successful.
- Wealthy people recognise that no matter how old, wise or experienced you get, you can never learn enough. As such, wealthy people are always learning. They devour

all that they can and they take what they learn and put it into action to test it's effectiveness for themselves.
- This desire to learn more is driven by an intense curiosity. Even the most successful people in the world continually look for new and innovative ways to make money or do business.
- Wealthy people avoid distraction when they are working because they understand the importance of focus. Focus is essential to getting things done efficiently.
- Talking of focus, wealthy people do not waste time doing lots of projects spreading themselves too thinly. They work smart rather than hard by getting rid of infective projects and only working on things which bring maximum results. At the same time, they recognise that there is an opportunity cost for every choice you make in life. This means that they recognise that sometimes, sacrifices need to be made and are prepared to work hard in order to achieve success.
- It takes discipline and focus to become wealthy. The majority of people lack self-control. In order to become wealthy, you must have self-control or the ability to delay gratification. The wealthy are usually incredibly disciplined.
- Wealthy people are well organised in all aspects of their life. This includes paying bills. They always pay on time and never incur late fees. They maximise their time at

work by focusing on what is important so that they can have time for things other than work.

- Wealthy people are open minded, flexible and accepting of change. They embrace change, especially if it is something which will benefit their business. In a world in which technology moves at such an astounding rate, this is an essential trait for any person in business.
- They make the act of making money and keeping money seem as easy as breathing! They usually have everything they want, so they tend to spend less than "poor people," meaning that they easily save more.
- They have a lot of financial knowledge and keep abreast of what is going on in the financial world. Having financial knowledge is essential if you are to have money and hold onto it. If they do not have a lot of financial knowledge, they pay for the services of those that do.
- The wealthy are able to identify their strengths and weaknesses with confidence. This means that they are acutely aware of the things they are good at and of the things they are bad at. This enables them to compensate for weaknesses by either training in that area or hiring an expert. The ability to reflect in this way is so important to financial decision making and awareness as well as a whole host of other things which are necessary to build wealth.
- High achievers often know exactly what they will be

doing in the short, medium and long term. They set goals for themselves and they put things in place to ensure they achieve those goals. They lay out a clear road map to success and they follow that map diligently.

In conclusion, when searching for a millionaire you need to understand their habits, trait and wants. This will give you better chances and edge to outsmart your fellow suitor.

KIM REINVENTED HERSELF WITH THE SOLE AIM OF LANDING A RICH HUSBAND - AND GOT ONE

Don't only read the story below for fun but let it motivate you. No matter the age, in as much you still fall within the age range and you can work on yourself better like Kim, definitely your millionaire husband is right behind the corner. But don't get it twisted there are some age range mentioned in this guide that will be very difficult for you to continue with the goal of chasing a millionaire husband. Read this story and see how she gets it done!

Last spring, I flew to New York for a date with a man I had not met before. As I walked towards the arrivals lounge I frantically smoothed down my clothes, fretting that my carefully selected wardrobe (Moschino shirt, Mulberry holdall and fake-but-convincing diamond earrings) wouldn't be showy enough to impress an American multi-millionaire.

This, after all, was a man who owned a penthouse in Florida, a ski lodge in Colorado and a business pad in New York. He ate in top restaurants, drank the finest champagnes and, I was sure, could have dated any woman he set his sights on.

But he wasn't dating any woman, he was dating me — a pharmacy counter saleswoman from the dull old town of Brigg in North Lincolnshire. And, yes, I'd targeted him not just because he was attractive, but also because he had serious money.

The simple fact is, I'd spent months changing my appearance, and even my accent, all so I would meet a rich man. And if that sounds shallow, then let me explain a little about my past.

I come from a very humble background and left school with no qualifications. I

married my boyfriend Steven, a mechanic, straight out of school and, aged 20, gave birth to our daughter Claudia.

I worked in my local pharmacy, but I always felt I deserved a better life. Just like people who believe they have been born the wrong gender or in the wrong era, I felt like I'd been born into the wrong social class.

I had this hunger for the finer things in life, and the lives I read about in glossy magazines. I wanted to live in beautiful houses and own designer clothes and jewellery.

Although people always describe me as good-looking, I dreamt of having a nose job and a boob job. If I really wanted to live this life I dreamed of, it was obvious that my next partner would need to have money. Proper money.

So when my marriage fizzled out and I found myself nudging 40, I decided to reinvent myself into the kind of woman that a wealthy man might find attractive. But how could a beauty counter assistant from Brigg pull it off?

In my head, I made a mental list of how I would go about it. No man is going to look at a woman he believes is simply after his money, so I had to pretend I had my own. The first thing that had to go was my Northern accent. I'd always hated the way people from Brigg said 'ey up' or referred to me as 'our Kim'. Northern accents make people assume you're stupid and working class. I needed to delete my past in order to change my future.

First, I decided to invest in elocution lessons. I spent £600 seeing a private tutor twice a week. After six months, it was virtually impossible to tell I had been born in the North.

Secondly, I needed to know where rich people ate, and

where they holidayed. I needed to educate myself.

I read glossy magazines to find out about the best restaurants and the most luxurious resorts, and I got books from the library on etiquette. I didn't want to use the wrong knife or pick up someone else's bread roll by mistake. I remember one book said it was OK to get your compact out at the table because the Queen does that. I do that all the time now.

If I was going to convince someone that I had the same life as them — and, more importantly, that I could fit into their world — I needed to know the places that they were talking about, and exactly how to behave.

Finally, I knew I had to look the part. It's no good having a beautiful voice if you're dressed head-to-toe in High Street clothes.

Here, though, I had a problem. I'd already spent my savings on elocution lessons: how could I afford a whole new wardrobe — and a designer one at that — on my meagre wage?

But I wasn't about to give up. I took on as many extra

shifts as I could manage, and saved every last penny. Instead of buying from designer shops, I spent hours scouring eBay.

I decided that I would focus on building up an expensive look to be worn only on dates. I bought a second-hand Mandalay dress (sexy but classy), plus a few designer accessories, including a second-hand Christian Dior bag and a Louis Vuitton holdall. I also bought a crisp Moschino shirt and some well-cut Joe's Jeans for a more casual look.

It didn't matter when I needed to default on my electricity bill so I could afford hair extensions. I was speculating to accumulate — and I knew it would be worth it.

Within a year, I'd completely transformed myself. Friends I hadn't seen in months didn't recognise me. But where to start my search for a rich man? By chance, I'd heard about a dating website called iloveyouraccent.com and at first I thought it was something to do with having a nice voice. But when I looked into it, it turned out to specialise in introducing American men and women to potential partners in Britain.

Suddenly, everything just seemed to slot into place. To put it simply, I knew it would be easier to reinvent myself if there was a bit of distance between my past life and what I hoped would be my future life — a life with a wealthy American.

On my profile, I described myself as a 'fun-loving, sophisticated woman', and said that I was looking for a man who liked 'the finer things in life'. Obviously I didn't say that I was looking for someone with money, because that would have put people off, but I hoped it was clear all the same. And that's how I found David. From the moment I spoke to him, I knew he was the one for me.

I'd had a few emails from other men, but as a general rule, if a man talks to you mainly about sport and alcohol then he hasn't got much else going on in his life. David peppered his emails to me with tales of flying business class and expensive champagnes. I knew he had to have serious money. This was the man I had been waiting for.

What did I tell him about me? Not very much during those early conversations. I described my job as being for a 'cosmetics house' (rather than a local pharmacy) and didn't give away too much about my background.

So for weeks I sent these vague emails, giving him very little information about me but finding out more and more about his life. He owned his own business and took five-star holidays in the Caribbean. I was thrilled when he asked me to meet him for a date in New York.

There was just one problem: there was no way I could afford the flight, and no way I could tell him the truth about my finances.

Instead I stalled, telling him that I had work commitments. It worked. Before long, he had

bought me a business-class ticket and offered to pay for the hotel.

It was a magical five days. The last time I'd been to America, I'd been eyeing up $50 fake designer handbags. This time we stayed at the Waldorf Astoria, where David had booked us separate rooms, so there was no pressure to sleep together.

We spent the next few days going to galleries and designer clothes shops and eating at the most wonderful restaurants. And on the final night, we slept together — not least because, by then, I found David irresistible.

I remember vividly that his last words before I got on the plane back to London were 'Bye, sweetie', which really worried me. It sounded as though I might be nothing more than a good-looking distraction.

Back in the UK, however, there were beautiful flowers and a card waiting for me, telling me what a great time he'd had. And from there, the relationship became very intense very quickly. We'd talk on the phone six or seven times a day, and David was always sending me huge bouquets of flowers.

Just three months later, he asked me to marry him and move out to America. I didn't hesitate. By then, I was head over heels in love. My friends and family were shocked that I would so readily give up my life — but that had always been my plan. If you settle for the mundane, then that's how your life will be. Instead, I identified my dream life and had been determined to get it.

In August last year, David and I got married in his Florida apartment and spent our honeymoon travelling around the Caribbean (Jamaica, St Lucia, St Martin...). Only a handful of his family were present at the wedding, plus a few of my really good friends and one of my favourite aunts.

Yes, it's fair to say that a lot of people from my old life thought I was being cold and calculating, and they didn't want to support me — but I can live with that. A month before we got married, I did take David back to Brigg to show him where I came from, and at that point I was a little more open with him about my background.

David's only comment was: 'Let's get out of here!' He still doesn't know exactly how close to the breadline I've been — though I did confess that I'd changed certain things about myself to attract him, and he thinks that's funny. Americans are generally more comfortable with the idea of bettering yourself than British people are.

Now, really I'm living the dream, and I have to pinch myself every morning to remind myself that I've actually been this lucky. My life now consists of shopping, then going to the gym or for lunch. David's helping me set up a little fake-tanning business to keep me occupied, because there is only so much shopping you can do!

Apart from my gorgeous husband and our lovely homes, I've got a beautiful white Mercedes to drive and a closet full of amazing clothes, not to mention a diamond bracelet and Rolex watch. Do I feel like I'm still playing a part? In some ways, yes I do. I'm still careful to keep things vague when I talk to people about my background.

And do people back home who know the whole story think I'm a gold-digger? Well yes, of course, some of them do. But I'm not interested in what other people think. I would recommend what I've done to any woman who is in a rut and really committed to pulling herself out of it. Just look at my life: you could do the same.

David and I have been together for nine months and we are totally happy in each other's company. He's got that lovely quiet confidence which people who are comfortable around wealth have, and it's very, very sexy.

He didn't even demand a pre-nup when we got married. And for my part, I told him that if, after a few months, things weren't working out, then I'd go back to England with nothing more than I left with. But can I really see myself going back to the life I had in Lincolnshire? Not for a minute.

Lessons

Kim's story makes us understand no matter your background and where you come from, if you dream of getting married to a millionaire it will definitely come through. Though it wasn't an easy task for Kim but she never gave up. She worked on her body physique, and shopped for the latest dresses to make her looks sexy. She Understood the rules and stayed focused despite distractions from many men. You can also emulate the story of Kim by following do's and don't mentioned in thise book.

What Are the Goal Setting to Marry a Millionaire

The majority of people are not wealthy simply because they do not set themselves clear goals. Remember, as we saw in the last chapter, the wealthy are in fact in the minority, even in the richest nations on Earth. The wealthy on the other hand, understand that in order to achieve anything, they must set goals so that they can create a kind of road map to help them to achieve those goals.

If you spend your life having wishy washy aspirations such as "I want to be happy," or the classic one, "I just want more money," how on Earth do you expect to get anywhere by making generalised statements of what you think you want? How can you possibly make more money if you do not know how much money you want? How can you be happy if you do not know what will make you happy?

Definition of a Goal

A goal is a clearly defined objective. For example, a wealthy person would not just say that they want more money, they would know exactly how much money they want AND by what date they want it! Once you set yourself a clearly defined objective like that, you can then lay out all of the things you must do in order to make X amount of money in say six months' time. It is a very simple concept, but it is extremely powerful because it forces you to focus on what needs to be done in order to achieve your desired outcome.

Let me give you a real life example of how this would work. If you were overweight and needed to loose some weight, the strategy you would use to loose 20 pounds would be completely different to the strategy you would use to loose 60 pounds. Let's look more closely at this.

o   **20 pound strategy**

If your goal was to loose 20 pounds within 4 months, you might employ the following strategies:

1. Cut out on chocolate and sweets during the week.
2. Replace all unhealthy snacks with healthy snacks like fruit.
3. Drink at least 1.5 litres of water a day.
4. Join an exercise class for one hour, three times a week.

By doing this, you could easily loose 20 pounds the allotted time, but there is no way you could employ the same strategy to loose 60 pounds in that time.

o   **60 pound strategy**

If your goal was to loose 60 pounds in four months you might employ the following strategies:

1. Cut out all starchy foods.
2. Cut out all sugary foods.
3. Cut out all processed foods.
4. Eat lean meat, fruits and vegetables.
5. Replace your evening meal with a slimming protein

shake.
6. Drink at least 1.5 litres of water a day.
7. Join a gym and employ a personal trainer.
8. Exercise at least four times a week for an hour each time.

By employing the above Eight strategies and sticking to them diligently, you could easily surpass your goal of loosing 60 pounds in four months.

Now can you see why setting goals are critical to your success? When you set yourself goals which seem high, your unconscious mind is forced to come up with the appropriate strategies to get there. If you set low goals, well your mind will be forced to come up with the appropriate strategies to get there also. If you want mediocrity, that is fine, but if you want excellence, state it and put the strategies in place to achieve it, but be precise. The goal determines the strategy; however, if you set the wrong strategy, you will end up with the wrong result. Ensure that your strategy is well thought through and appropriate for your goal.

- **Be SMART**

In marketing, there is an acronym for goal setting called setting SMART objectives. SMART stands for:

- **S**= Specific
- **M**= Measurable
- **A**= Achievable

- **R**= Realistic
- **T**= Time bound

All pretty self-explanatory, but in my view, no goal is unrealistic or unachievable. All that is required is the right strategy. If you decide you want to meet your millionaire future husband within six months, you can do it, but you need the right strategy to get there.

Once your strategies are in place, you must follow through with persistent and decisive action. Visualise yourself achieving your goal. Visualise the life you will have with your husband in five years' time and focus on what that might feel like! Make those feelings live in you every day. This feeling will be the fuel that drives you to act decisively, working your way through all of your strategies diligently until you have met him.

Do not have wishy washy goals which you have no control over. The following are wishy washy, useless goals:

- The wish to have a loving marriage.
- The wish to have successful and happy children.
- The wish to be fulfilled.

All of them are useless in the grand scheme of things. You cannot strategize your way to having a loving marriage any more than you can strategize your way to being fulfilled! Get the picture? There is nothing wrong with wanting these abstract things, just understand that they are not goals.

Now you have all of the information you need to find yourself a millionaire to love. The steps discussed in this book which you need to follow are summarised below, along with some useful tips. Recognise that this is not an easy path to follow. It takes dedication and hard work, but it is not impossible.

Before you go ahead, take a good look inside yourself and decide whether or not this is truly what you want. Seriously consider the possibility of making a lot of money yourself, it is probably a lot easier than trying to leverage someone else's money through marriage.

Understand that you can do anything you put your mind to. You could go back to school and learn something which will help you to get a better job or you could set up your own business. If you are relatively young, take this into consideration.

No matter how much or how little money you make, save some money every single month. Even if it is a tiny amount, it will build up. Above all, never give up on the possibility of finding true and lasting love. Just because it might be with a rich man, does not mean that it cannot be real!

Assuming you have thought through all of these things and still want to go ahead, read on.

WOMAN MARRIES ONLINE BOYFRIEND WITHIN 10MONTHS AND FINDS OUT HE'S A MILLIONAIRE

Reading this story doesn't mean every woman will find her potential millionaire husband online or any social network platform, but it's to make you believe and understand that you can find them anywhere. The case of Nguyen Van Anh who of course luckily found her millionaire husband on facebook.

The presence of social network sites makes it possible for people to interact with each other from different parts of the world and yet, many people still frown at such relationships. However, many marriages have blossomed from online for many years and this was the case for Nguyen Van Anh, a Vietnamese woman who found out her online boyfriend's real identity and economic status during their marriage preparations.

It was in May 2016, while Van Anh scanned through the Facebook page of her idol, her attention was struck by a vague image of a man in the background. Her curiosity, made Van Anh to send a message to her Idol asking to be introduced to the mystery guy.

Even though her Idol was not really close to the gentleman, the latter gave in to the woman's request and connected the two on social media. The mystery man later turned out to be Dang Tuan, who immediately got in touch with Van Anh. The two formed a connection and started dating.

Their relationship blossomed even though it was a long distance where she lived in Hanoi, Vietnam while Dang was living and working in Russia. After ten months of dating, Dang Tuan asked for her hand in marriage, which she agreed to.

But, Van Anh's mother was not pleased with daughter's choice and she warned her about the regrets that could come from

dating someone she met online and has not taken time to know.

Dang was not put off by this. He traveled all the way to Vietnam to prove his love for Van Anh to her parents.

After, persistent convincing, the parents accepted to give the couple their blessing.

The couple travelled to Russia during the wedding preparations and that's when Van Anh learnt that her seemingly humble fiance was a rich general manager of a Fashion Brand.

He confessed that he had kept his money a secret because he wanted a woman who loved him for him and not only for money.

The two got married last year in April and have been blessed with a baby. Van Anh relocated to Russia where they now live as a family.

Lessons

Van Anh's success story was possible because at first she believed in love and good personalty. The lesson from this beautiful story are:

o   Don't let your ego overshadow your goals
o   Never say never!
o   Believe in your dream
o   Work on your beauty and physique.

Steps to Marrying a Millionaire

o **Honestly look at yourself and evaluate what you have.**

Do you have the required looks and personality? If the answer is no and you cannot realistically improve yourself to the required standard, consider giving up now to save yourself the trouble.

o **Assuming you have the basics, change what needs to be changed.**

Work hard on improving your body, your personal grooming and education. Make sure you look the part AND have the personality traits to match. Give yourself time to really develop. Only go out looking for your future mate once you are on top of your game.

o **Learn about the things that the wealthy are into.**

Learn about fine wines, fine dining, golf, horse riding, skiing. You get the picture. Learn about all of the classic accessories and cars of the wealthy so that you can spot them.

o **Go to the same places as the wealthy.**

Eat where they eat, club where they club. Work where they work. Spend time with them. Join millionaire dating sites if necessary.

Take an equally well groomed friend when you are going out to eat or socialise with the wealthy. Do not take any friend, male or female who is not up to the same standard as you physically and intellectually. Your friend should be classy and subtle, just like you.

Learn etiquette. Get elocution lessons if necessary.

- **Be alert at all times and never talk about money.**

Even if your future partner brings the subject up, act nonchalant, as if it is not important. Wear a pleasant, but slightly uninterested smile.

If you are a woman, realistically speaking, you have a limited time in which to attract a wealthy man, 10 to 15 years tops. Unfortunately, in most cases, this is the reality. If this is something you really want to do, do it while you are young. It is a little easier for men, so if you are a guy, you have more time, but it is a little more difficult to find and marry a wealthy woman than it is for a young woman to find and marry a wealthy man.

- **It is a good idea to meet a millionaire when they are young and single.**

Flashy bling types are probably not a good idea as they are unlikely to be stable. If you are going for a young millionaire, pay attention to the quiet shy types as they are likely to be much more reliable and sensible.

- **Do not swear, do not do drugs and do not drink to excess.**

In fact, if any of these are your habits and you plan on marrying into money, I would advise you to cut them out now, while you are working on yourself. Remember, habits which are practised every day eventually become a part of your behaviour. Eliminate bad habits and improve your behaviour for the better.

- **Remember that the wealthy are very careful in who they select as mates.**

Men want well bred, attractive and intelligent women who make them look good and women want the same. Be acutely aware of this at all times and act accordingly.

- **Do not show too much skin and definitely do not get huge breast implants.**

You must make yourself look and act like a potential wife, not a porn star.

- **Get rid of any piercings and do not get any tattoos.**

If you already have tattoos, consider having them removed.

- **If you are a woman, your make-up should be expertly applied but it should also be subtle. Less is more.**
- **Get a classy hair cut with subtle highlights.**

If you dye your hair, ensure the colour is natural looking and touch up the roots regularly.

- **Only wear subtle jewellery.**
- **If you are a woman, channel someone like Princess Grace Kelly in your persona! Be a lady at all times. Remember your etiquettes always.**

Your clothes should be made of natural materials, not synthetic materials - cotton, wool, cashmere and silk. All of these are classy materials. Do not wear bright and garish colours. Reserve bright colours for elegant evening wear on certain occasions.

- **Do not wear clothes with huge obvious designer labels.**

Invest in a few choice classic garments specifically for your dates. Build your wardrobe slowly. Consider visiting charity stores in wealthy areas or websites like eBay for discount but classy designer items which look the part and fit you well. Your clothes should be well tailored if possible. Consider taking any classy items which are not well tailored to a seamstress for tailoring.

- Do NOT attempt to get pregnant in order to trap a wealthy man. You will only land yourself in big trouble.
- Do not accept expensive gifts until you are engaged. By doing so, he may loose respect for you as it will look as if

you are easily bought!
- NEVER talk about commitment or try to force him into any form of commitment. As with most men, this will only cause him to back away from you. The same applies to men dating wealthy women. You want to foster trust, not suspicion. Ladies, if he does not ask for your hand after five years of courtship, he probably never will, so leave him.
- Make your partner wait for sex. Having sex too soon is a mine field.
- Perfect the art of being a good lover, so that when that special time does come, he or she will know that it was worth the wait.
- Stay away from married wealthy people!
- Do not go after the relatives or friends of the person you are dating! That is just not polite!
- Learn how to cook gourmet food and learn how to cook it well. Spoil your partner with delicious food and demonstrate your knowledge of the finer things in life.
- If you have children, only date men or women who like children.
- Steer clear of those who are not wealthy.

PS: I hope you enjoyed reading the book and found it beneficial. I will appreciate if you will please review the book for benefit of the other readers.

Grab other Books by the Author

How to Marry a Millionaire

Stop the Clock: Can we Live Longer by Reversing Aging Process?

Stop the Clock: Anti-Aging Beauty Secrets Revealed

Stop the Clock: How to Improve Your Physical, Mental & Sexual Energy with Age?

About The Author

Rachita Kumar is Bachelor of Science in Nutrition and Child Psychology. Since leaving college she has been keenly interested in science of anti-aging and how by eating correct foods you can slow the aging process in the body and skin. She writes books and articles on anti-aging, nutrition, health and women's issues.

For more information on anti-aging, nutrition and health issues visit her website **Healthy Wise Choice** (http://healthywisechoice.com/)

Rachita's husband Praveen is an investor, business builder and a best-selling author who has helped hundreds of people to get started on their journey to create sustainable wealth with minimum risk. You can visit his Wealth Creation Academy website (https://wealth-creation-academy.com) for more information on accelerated wealth creation strategies that will help you obtain financial freedom within a very short time frame.

Disclaimer

The advice contained in this material might not be suitable for everyone. The author obtained the information from sources believed to be reliable and from his own personal experience, but he neither implies nor intends any guarantee of accuracy.

The author, publisher and distributors never give legal, accounting, medical or any other type of professional advice. The reader must always seek those services from competent professionals that can review their own particular circumstances.

The author, publisher and distributors particularly disclaim any liability, loss, or risk taken by individuals who directly or indirectly act on the information contained herein. All readers must accept full responsibility for their use of this material.

All pictures used in this book are for illustrative purposes only. The people in the pictures are not connected with the book, author or publisher and no link or endorsement between any of them and the topic or content is implied, nor should any be assumed. The pictures are only licensed for use in this book and must not be used for any other purpose without prior written permission of the rights holder.

Printed by Libri Plureos GmbH in Hamburg, Germany